BELIEVING
GOD

Devotional Journal

BELIEVING GOD

Devotional Journal

BETH MOORE

Nashville, Tennessee

BELIEVING GOD DEVOTIONAL JOURNAL
Copyright © 2004 by Beth Moore
All rights reserved

Broadman & Holman Publishers
Nashville, Tennessee
www.broadmanholman.com

ISBN 0-8054-3190-X

Edited by Dale McCleskey

Unless otherwise indicated, all Scripture quotations are taken from the
Holy Bible, New International Version, Copyright © 1973, 1978, 1984 by the
International Bible Society. Used by permission of Zondervan Bible Publishers.

Dewey Decimal Classification: 242.64
Subject Heading: God \ Christian Life \ Devotional Literature

Printed in the United States
1 2 3 4 07 06 05 04

Dedication

Having dedicated the original message by the same title to my dear church, it is only fitting that I dedicate this companion journal to my beloved Sunday School class.

To the wonderful people of Water's Edge class.
You are the hug of God to me. I'm nuts about you.

Love, Beth

Table of Contents

4. I CAN DO ALL THINGS THROUGH CHRIST

5. GOD'S WORD IS ALIVE AND ACTIVE IN ME

$\jmath$ntroduction

I am totally convinced that nothing is more valuable in our lives than time spent quietly with God. Everything else flows from this deliberate experience of sitting with Him, reading His Word, hearing His heart, and rising up to live what we believe. From our marriages and families to our jobs and daily responsibilities, everything of value to us is charged with new meaning by the time we spend letting God teach us who He is—and who we are as a result of His limitless grace.

The thing I love about this journaling format is that it gives you time to slow down and chew on each word of Scripture, to listen in an unhurried fashion, and to let both the demands and blessings of belief sink deeply into your heart. I pray this is going to be a life-changing experience for you, and I am so glad you've chosen to embark on it with me.

Even though there's more than one way for you to use and benefit from this book, let me tell you real quickly how it's set up. The outline for this journal is taken from the pledge of faith I talked about in the *Believing God* book and study course—which you're hopefully already familiar with:

- God is who He says He is,
- God can do what He says He can do,
- I am who God says I am,
- I can do all things through Christ,
- God's Word is alive and active in me.

These five statements encompass virtually everything we're challenged to believe. They are the simple answer to just about any temptation you will ever face.

Each devotional experience covers four pages, although you don't have to worry about completing them all at one sitting. Each includes a combination of Scripture, meditations, and journaling starters. And at the end of each devotion, you'll have a chance to write out your own prayers, letting God's Word become more than words on a page but the offering of Your lips in praise and in need of God.

In between each section, I've also given you lots of room to record "Godstops." These are simply the daily, ongoing moments in your life when you recognize the fingerprints of God on a particular situation, a certain occurrence, or perhaps just a thought He sent sailing into your head. The "stop" part of the word is an acronym, meaning "Savoring The Observable Presence." Because so many things slip by us unnoticed in an average day, we miss most of His work unless we force ourselves to pay attention to it. The way I look at it—if God loves me enough to reveal Himself to me, I don't want to miss anything He may be saying. I want it all! And "Godstops" provide a great way to keep track of them.

My prayer is that this journal will transform your belief in God from a mere noun into a new spiritual grammar that covers all the parts of speech—action, description, being, and detail. May we ever encourage one another to lose ourselves in *Believing God*.

Love, Beth

Section One

GOD IS WHO HE SAYS HE IS

You know that it was not with perishable things such as silver or gold that you were redeemed from the empty way of life handed down to you from your forefathers, but with the precious blood of Christ, a lamb without blemish or defect. . . . Through him you believe in God, who raised him from the dead and glorified him, and so your faith and hope are in God.

—*1 Peter 1:18-19, 21*

IT'S WHO YOU KNOW

 Know that the LORD is God. It is he who made us, and we are his; we are his people, the sheep of his pasture. Enter his gates with thanksgiving and his courts with praise; give thanks to him and praise his name.

—Psalm 100:3-4

Psalm 100:3 carries its own powerful punch that can easily be missed in the poetry: "Know that the LORD is God." Know above all else that YHWH, our covenant Maker, is Elohiym, the God over all creation.

In other words, you and I must "know"—not just hope or think—that the One who cut covenant with us through the torn flesh of Jesus Christ is the same One who sits upon the universe's throne, having spoken the worlds into existence. Surrounded by a society that spouts many gods, but at best nobly agrees to equate them, you and I can "*know* that the LORD is God."

Like you, perhaps, godless philosophies have never been my temptation. The most dangerously influential opinions in my life experience have been those held by intellectuals and scholars who profess Christianity but deny the truth and the present power of the Bible. Many of them believe God exists, but they teach that He is not exactly who Scripture says He is. Or they believe that He no longer does what Scripture says He can do.

It's not enough to merely hope we're on the right track. Hope alone will never dig a deep enough path to follow to our Promised Lands. Beloved, we're not going anywhere of profound eternal significance until we "know."

React to the Word

In Caesarea Philippi, Christ gathered His disciples around Him and asked these two vital questions that beg answers from us, as well. First, Christ asked, "Who do people say the Son of Man is?" (Matt. 16:13). What would you tell Him people are saying about God today?

_____

_____

_____

_____

_____

_____

_____

_____

_____

"But what about you?" he asked. "Who do you say I am?" (Matt. 16:15).

_____

_____

_____

_____

_____

_____

Reason with Your Heart

Why do all the worldly views about God make Him out to be less than He is?

How have you been able to deal with these ideas? How would you like to respond to those who challenge the notion that we can live with a vibrant, wholehearted belief in God?

How long will you waver between two opinions?
If the LORD is God, follow him.
—1 Kings 18:21

Respond with Prayer

Father, so often I feel like the man who exclaimed, "I do believe!" then in a flood of sincerity cried out, "Help me overcome my unbelief!" (Mark 9:24). Please help me overcome my own unbelief, Lord, so I can start taking You at Your Word, coming to know You in such depth that . . .

_____

_____

_____

_____

_____

_____

_____

_____

_____

_____

_____

_____

_____

_____

_____

_____

_____

_____

You of little faith, why are you so afraid?
—Matthew 8:26

PAST PERFECT

*In the future, when your children ask you, "What do these
stones mean?" tell them that the flow of the Jordan was cut off
before the ark of the covenant of the LORD. When it crossed
the Jordan, the waters of the Jordan were cut off. These stones
are to be a memorial to the people of Israel forever.*

—Joshua 4:6-7

God never forgets His promises to us. In turn, He intends for His children
never to forget His faithfulness, never to doubt that He will fulfill the promises He has made in His Word.

Over and over in Scripture, God's people are told to actively remember all
He has done in their behalf. Intentionally remembering how God has worked
in our past provides a powerful motivation for believing God in our present.

I've made memories with my family, of course, that will be engraved on
my mind forever. My relationship with God, however, preceded my present
family. My longest and most effective history with anyone has been with God
Himself. I received Christ as my Savior in childhood and have loved Him
longer, known Him better, and experienced life with Him more intimately
than anyone else.

You don't have to know God long to make memories with Him. The more
you look back, the more you can see that He was always at work, long before
you accepted His Son as your Savior. Actively remembering His faithfulness
yesterday will greatly increase your willingness to trust Him today.

React to the Word

"They believed his promises and sang his praise. But they soon forgot what he had done and did not wait for his counsel" (Ps. 106:12-13). Israel's seasons of rebellion were often matters of forgetfulness. What have you forgotten of His faithfulness, and how has it affected your relationship with Him?

_____

_____

_____

_____

_____

_____

_____

_____

_____

_____

_____

_____

_____

_____

_____

_____

_____

_____

_____

_____

_____

_____

Reason with Your Heart

Think about how you can leave your children and descendants—whether physical or spiritual—a record of their lineage and heritage of faith. How would you start? What would you include? Begin your ideas . . .

_____

_____

_____

_____

_____

_____

_____

_____

_____

_____

_____

_____

_____

_____

_____

_____

_____

_____

_____

_____

I will remember the deeds of the LORD;
yes, I will remember your miracles of long ago.
—Psalm 77:11

Respond with Prayer

Father, help me not to be like the ancient Israelites who willfully put You to the test (Ps. 78:18). They did not believe in You or trust in Your deliverance even after all the wonders You had shown them (Ps. 78:22). Please swell my soul with belief. Help me to trust emphatically in You—to trust you for . . .

_____

_____

_____

_____

_____

_____

_____

_____

_____

_____

_____

_____

_____

_____

_____

_____

_____

_____

The Holy Spirit . . . will remind you
of everything I have said to you.
—John 14:26

BECAUSE OF UNBELIEF

 With whom was he angry for forty years? Was it not with those who sinned, whose bodies fell in the desert? And to whom did God swear that they would never enter his rest if not to those who disobeyed? So we see that they were not able to enter, because of their unbelief.

—Hebrews 3:17–19

Why isn't our present practice of Christianity working, and why don't we see more of God's promises fulfilled? I believe it's the same reason the practices of the Israelites in the wilderness didn't work.

Like them, we can be dramatically delivered from bondage, leave our Egypts, and yet never make it to our Promised Lands. We, too, can find ourselves lodged in a desolate wilderness between slavery and freedom. Hebrews 3:19 supplies the one-word explanation: "They were not able to enter, because of their unbelief." Oh, they believed in God, but they didn't believe the God they believed in.

The question raised in the wilderness wanderings was not whether the Israelites belonged to God or where they would spend eternity. The question was—where would the chosen people of God spend their earthly existence? We can be safely tucked in the family of God and have the full assurance of a heavenly inheritance without ever occupying the land of God's fulfilled promises on earth. The Israelites of the Exodus were promised many things. But the masses never saw their theology become a reality.

React to the Word

Romans 11:20 tells us that Israel as a nation has been broken off from God for a time because of unbelief. If unbelief has such devastating consequences, how should we react to our tendency to disbelieve God? What consequences has it already caused you, your church, or your family?

_____

_____

_____

_____

_____

_____

_____

_____

_____

_____

_____

_____

_____

_____

_____

_____

_____

_____

_____

Reason with Your Heart

How would you describe to a new believer the difference between believing in God and really believing God?

_____

_____

_____

_____

_____

_____

_____

_____

_____

In what areas do you find believing God most difficult?

_____

_____

_____

_____

_____

_____

_____

_____

_____

Today, if you hear his voice, do not harden
your hearts as you did in the rebellion.
—Hebrews 3:15

Respond with Prayer

Father, I want You to be able to look at my life as You did Stephen's, and be able to say that I am full of the Holy Spirit and faith, and that many people were brought to the Lord through my witness (Acts 11:24). Help me see that faith in You has the power to . . .

_____

_____

_____

_____

_____

_____

_____

_____

_____

_____

_____

_____

_____

_____

_____

_____

_____

_____

_____

_____

*If they do not persist in unbelief, they will be
grafted in, for God is able to graft them in again.*
—*Romans 11:23*

GOD IS SO GOOD

 You greatly rejoice, though now for a little while you may have had to suffer grief in all kinds of trials. These have come so that your faith—of greater worth than gold, which perishes even though refined by fire—may be proved genuine and may result in praise, glory and honor when Jesus Christ is revealed.

—1 Peter 1:6-7

We may as well accept faith challenges as a fact of life and not be shocked or feel picked on when they come. God brings them to build our faith, prove us genuine, and afford Himself endless excuses to reward us. He delights in nothing more than our choice to believe Him over what we see and feel. Our ultimate purpose for existence is to please God; therefore, if we don't exercise faith, we will never fulfill our reason for being.

If you haven't yet developed a trust relationship with God, this concept of living your entire life to please Someone else may unnerve or even offend you. I understand this, because I, too, have battled tremendous trust issues. I have not always found man nor myself trustworthy, but God has never failed to live up to His Word in our relationship.

God is for us, dear one. Even His commands are for our safety, liberty, and blessing. Yes, He calls us to surrender our own agendas on the altar of His will, but Romans 12:2 reminds us that God's will is good, pleasing, and perfectly suited for us. Ultimately, the biggest sacrifices of our lives will have been the times we chose our own way and forfeited His pleasing will for us.

React to the Word

After delivering the Law to Moses, God told him to command and encourage the people "to observe the LORD's commands and decrees that I am giving you today for your own good" (Deut. 10:13). In what sense do you see that God's commands are always for our good?

_____

_____

_____

_____

_____

_____

_____

_____

_____

_____

_____

_____

_____

_____

_____

_____

_____

_____

_____

_____

_____

_____

_____

Reason with Your Heart

What have you ever sacrificed by choosing your own way rather than God's?

How does Satan try to persuade you toward unbelief and disobedience? Not just people in general, but how does he personalize his attacks on you?

He gave them their request, but sent leanness into their soul.
—Psalm 106:15 (KJV)

Respond with Prayer

Show me Your ways, O Lord, and teach me Your paths. Guide me in Your truth and teach me, for You are God my Savior, and my hope is in You all day long (Ps. 25:4-5). Remind me of the benefits that come from believing You and the losses that result from unbelief . . .

_____

_____

_____

_____

_____

_____

_____

_____

_____

_____

_____

_____

_____

_____

_____

_____

_____

_____

I trust that you will discover that we have not failed the test.

—2 Corinthians 13:6

BIG GOD

"All the arrogant and every evildoer will be stubble, and
that day that is coming will set them on fire," says the LORD
Almighty. . . . "But for you who revere my name, the sun of
righteousness will rise with healing in its wings. And you
will go out and leap like calves released from the stall."
—Malachi 4:1-2

All human attempts to define God cannot help but minimize Him. We try
to make God behave and fit into our textbooks. We want Him to calm down
and not be so . . . God-ish. We decide we will only believe what we can
humanly reconcile.

But all attempts to take away the mystery and wonder that surround God
leave Him being pictured as something He is not. We cannot tame the Lion
of Judah. There is a mystery, a wonder, and, yes, even a wildness about God
we cannot take from Him. Nor would we want to take it away—even if it
would enable us to fully, humanly grasp the adventure of Him.

We must beware of recreating an image of God that makes us feel better
about ourselves or puffs our desperate, prideful desire to feel smarter than we
are. If we can come up with a God we can fully explain, we have come up
with a different God than the Bible's.

Of this I'm certain: if in our pursuit of greater knowledge, God seems to
have gotten smaller, we have been deceived. I don't care how intelligent the
deceiver seems or how well-meaning and sincere his or her doctrine is.

React to the Word

Feast your eyes on the incredible portrait of the risen Christ found in Revelation 1:12-16—"like blazing fire . . . like bronze glowing in a furnace . . . like the sound of rushing waters." What needs to happen in your life to enable you to experience His glory more often?

Reason with Your Heart

Name two or three people you know personally (or have known) whose view of God is bigger than most people's is.

_____

_____

_____

_____

_____

Describe what these individuals are like. How does their awe of God show itself in daily life? What would you give to be more in love with Him—like they are? To believe Him—like they do?

_____

_____

_____

_____

_____

_____

_____

_____

_____

_____

_____

Arise, shine, for your light has come,
and the glory of the LORD rises upon you.
—Isaiah 60:1

Respond with Prayer

Father, You are seated on a throne, high and exalted. The train of Your robe fills the temple. Above You are seraphs, calling to one another, "Holy, holy, holy is the LORD Almighty; the whole earth is full of his glory" (Isa. 6:1-3). May I see You each day as the powerful God You are . . .

_____

_____

_____

_____

_____

_____

_____

_____

_____

_____

_____

_____

_____

_____

_____

_____

_____

_____

To the King, eternal, immortal, invisible,
the only God, be honor and glory for ever and ever.
—1 Timothy 1:17

GodStops

"Savoring the Observable Presence"

These blank pages are all yours to help you see God at work in your life and around you in the world. Watch for glimpses of His presence in both the ordinary and the out-of-the-ordinary, through answered prayers and obvious interventions. Date them or mark them in some way to seal the experience, to help you return to these moments and see them in context.

Your entries do not need to be long and descriptive, unless that's your style. Short sentences and phrases can be quite sufficient. The goal is to take spiritual, ongoing notice of a God who is willingly, lovingly, and always at work in your life.

_____

_____

_____

_____

_____

_____

_____

_____

_____

_____

_____

_____

_____

Sing to him, sing praise to him; tell of all his wonderful acts.
—*Psalm 105:2*

_____

_____

_____

_____

_____

_____

_____

_____

_____

_____

_____

_____

_____

_____

_____

_____

_____

_____

_____

_____

_____

_____

_____

_____

_____

_____

_____

"Can anyone hide in secret places so that
I cannot see him?" declares the LORD.
—Jeremiah 23:24

He is not far from each one of us.

—Acts 17:27

Inscribe it on a scroll, that for the days
to come it may be an everlasting witness.
—Isaiah 30:8

Section Two

GOD CAN DO
WHAT HE SAYS
HE CAN DO

I am the LORD, and I will bring you out from under the yoke of the Egyptians. I will free you from being slaves to them, and I will redeem you with an outstretched arm and with mighty acts of judgment. . . . And I will bring you to the land I swore with uplifted hand to give to Abraham, to Isaac, and to Jacob. I will give it to you as a possession. I am the LORD.

—Exodus 6:6, 8

EXTREME FAITH

 Faith is being sure of what we hope for and certain of what we do not see. This is what the ancients were commended for. . . . And without faith it is impossible to please God, because anyone who comes to him must believe that he exists and that he rewards those who earnestly seek him.

—Hebrews 11:1-2, 6

Two diametrically opposed teachings exist in the church today on the subject of faith and miracles: *cessationism* and *sensationalism*.

Simply put, cessationism teaches that dramatic miracles have ceased in our day. Sensationalism, on the other hand, teaches that miracles are the whole point of belief.

We must avoid the tendency to be drawn toward doctrinal extremes, many of which can be wildly offensive to God. Christ called those who didn't have enough miracle-believing faith an "unbelieving and perverse generation" (Luke 9:41), but he also called those who focused entirely on miracles a "wicked and adulterous generation" (Matthew 16:4).

I believe we can always hope and pray diligently for a miracle. The God we serve is able (Dan. 3:17), and everything is possible (Mark 9:23). If in His sovereignty God chooses to accomplish His purposes another way, we should still praise Him. Yet let it never be that we "have not" because we "ask not" (James 4:2, KJV) or because we don't believe in what God can do.

React to the Word

"And he will be called Wonderful" (Isa. 9:6). Full of wonders. Remove the wonders from God, and you can no longer call Him "Wonderful." Has God ceased to be wonderful to you? If so, how have you noticed this? If not, what has kept it from happening?

_____

_____

_____

_____

_____

_____

_____

_____

_____

_____

_____

_____

_____

_____

_____

_____

_____

_____

_____

_____

Reason with Your Heart

Which aspect do you find yourself drawn to: cessationism or sensationalism? Why does one come more naturally to you than another?

_____

_____

_____

_____

_____

_____

_____

What biblical ideas come to mind in supporting a balanced view of miracles that goes to neither extreme?

_____

_____

_____

_____

_____

_____

_____

_____

_____

I seek not to please myself but him who sent me.
—John 5:30

Respond with Prayer

Father God, You've told me that when I ask, I am to believe and not doubt, because he who doubts is like a wave of the sea, blown and tossed by the wind (James 1:6). Whenever I am tempted to doubt the intentions of Your heart and Your ability to do more than I can think or imagine, help me to . . .

_____

_____

_____

_____

_____

_____

_____

_____

_____

_____

_____

_____

_____

_____

_____

_____

_____

*For no matter how many promises God
has made, they are "Yes" in Christ.*
—2 *Corinthians 1:20*

BELIEVING FOR THE BEST

The father said to his servants, "Quick! Bring the best robe and put it on him. Put a ring on his finger and sandals on his feet. Bring the fattened calf and kill it. Let's have a feast and celebrate. For this son of mine was dead and is alive again; he was lost and is found." So they began to celebrate.

—Luke 15:22-24

I shamelessly ask God to bless my children. I ask Him to grant them health, joy, lasting romance with their life mates, laughter, lots of friends, and healthy, happy children. I also have no problem asking God if He might allow them to live in fairly close proximity so that I can rock my grandbabies often. I feel no conviction of sin over the temporal nature of these petitions.

As much as I hope God grants my children each of those things, however, these items do represent my "B" list. Among the things on my "A" list, I want my children to love God, revere His Word, and discover the life, healing, and power to be found within Him. I want them to love people and treat them with compassion and kindness. But more than anything on earth, I want glory to come to God through their lives.

I know I will never ask for more than God can supply, so I feel free to ask anything I desire for my loved ones. At the same time, God knows my absolute priorities for them. Therefore, if something on my "A" list temporarily—or even permanently (ouch!)—might have to cancel out something on my "B" list, so be it.

React to the Word

Hebrews 12:10 tells us God's intention for our lives: "Our fathers disciplined us for a little while as they thought best; but God disciplines us for our good, that we may share in his holiness." Why is sharing in God's holiness the very best opportunity we can be given in life?

_____

_____

_____

_____

_____

_____

_____

_____

_____

_____

_____

_____

_____

_____

_____

_____

_____

_____

_____

_____

Reason with Your Heart

What items make up your "A" list for your children or the other important people in your life?

_____

_____

_____

_____

_____

_____

_____

_____

_____

What goes on the "B" list you desire from the Lord? Does your list match the best your Father wants for you?

_____

_____

_____

_____

_____

_____

_____

_____

_____

_____

_____

How much more will your Father in heaven
give good gifts to those who ask him!
—Matthew 7:11

Respond with Prayer

Father, I pray that the eyes of my heart may be enlightened in order that I may know the hope to which You have called me, the riches of Your glorious inheritance in the saints, and Your incomparably great power for us who believe (Eph. 1:18-19). I feel free today to ask you . . .

_____

_____

_____

_____

_____

_____

_____

_____

_____

_____

_____

_____

_____

_____

_____

_____

_____

_____

_____

_____

_____

*How great is your goodness, which you
have stored up for those who fear you.*
—*Psalm 31:19*

ALL-OUT WAR

On the day the LORD gave the Amorites over to Israel, Joshua said to the LORD in the presence of Israel: "O sun, stand still over Gibeon, O moon, over the Valley of Aijalon." So the sun stood still, and the moon stopped, till the nation avenged itself on its enemies.

—Joshua 10:12-13

Sometimes God calls us to perseverance in seasons of sameness. At other times, we get change we don't want for reasons we don't like, and we'd give anything for life to go back to a daily routine. These are times when God seems to say, "I have a great victory in store for you, but if you want it, you'll have to give me nothing less than your all. It's going to take every bit of focus you've got, and you will literally live on my strength to get through it." In times like these, we can't even think about tomorrow, because we don't know how on earth we're going to live through the battle today.

Joshua faced that kind of challenge in this powerful scene from Israel's history. This wasn't a "be still" moment (Ps. 46:10). Nor was it a "stand still" moment (Ex. 14:14). It was a "wield your sword" moment that became a "one hundred percent, all you've got" moment.

God gave His fighting men an awesome victory, but He required every ounce of energy and cooperation they had in the process. Joshua didn't ask for the sun to stand still for nothing. He needed it that way because the time was growing slim, and the enemy was not yet conquered.

React to the Word

"There has never been a day like it before or since, a day when the LORD listened to a man" (Josh. 10:14). God hasn't stopped the sun in the sky for you, as He did for Joshua. But how has He shown you He listens to you?

_____

_____

_____

_____

_____

_____

_____

_____

_____

_____

_____

_____

_____

_____

_____

_____

_____

_____

_____

Reason with Your Heart

Fighting the fight of faith takes energy! But then, so does self-pity, anger, unforgiveness, and self-loathing. How can you decide where you're going to put your energy when the battle grows fierce?

_____

_____

_____

_____

_____

_____

_____

_____

_____

How does daily appropriating the grace of God prepare you for combat?

_____

_____

_____

_____

_____

_____

_____

_____

_____

See to it that no one misses the grace of God.
—Hebrews 12:15

Respond with Prayer

Lord, I don't want to waver through unbelief regarding Your promises, but I desire to be strengthened in my faith and give glory to You, God, being fully persuaded that You have power to do what You promise. You credit this kind of faith to Your children as righteousness (Rom. 4:22). Help me to draw all that I need from You . . .

_____

_____

_____

_____

_____

_____

_____

_____

_____

_____

_____

_____

_____

_____

_____

_____

Ah, Sovereign LORD . . . Nothing is too hard for you.
—Jeremiah 32:17

YES, I BELIEVE

We have heard with our ears, O God; our fathers have told us what you did in their days, in days long ago. . . . It was not by their sword that they won the land, nor did their arm bring them victory; it was your right hand, your arm, and the light of your face, for you loved them.

—Psalm 44:1, 3

If in reality we are seeing few wonders of God in the midst of His people, shouldn't we inquire as to why? Are we not desperate for it? Is God no longer willing to intervene miraculously and wondrously in our behalf?

We are surrounded by a dying and depraved world, mounting violence, the threat of mass destruction, disease, plague, enticing false religion, and a surging fury of satanic assault and seduction. We are desperate for the wonders and miracles of God. We need Him to show His mighty arm and tell the world that He is alive, active, and very much with us.

We are told that churches are in terrible decline. Many of today's pastors and leaders are depressed. Oppressed. Throngs of clueless people encircle us. We need more than the best programs and planning can accomplish. In fact, we need more than we even have the courage or imagination to ask.

Oh, that the church would fall on its face and cry out the words of the prophet Habakkuk: "LORD, I have heard of your fame; I stand in awe of your deeds, O LORD. Renew them in our day, in our time make them known" (Hab. 3:2).

React to the Word

Daniel's prayer is a reminder that God is in charge, He is active in our world, and His plans will prevail. "Praise be to the name of God for ever and ever; wisdom and power are his. He changes times and seasons; he sets up kings and deposes them" (Dan. 2:20-21). For what do you need to believe this today?

Reason with Your Heart

Name a miracle you would love to see God perform . . . maybe more than one . . . and all for His glory!

_____
_____
_____
_____
_____
_____
_____
_____

What kinds of miracles are already happening around you every day? They may seem little by some accounts, but they are of major importance to God.

_____
_____
_____
_____
_____
_____
_____
_____
_____

My ears had heard of you, but now my eyes have seen you.
—Job 42:5

Respond with Prayer

Lord, I want to be like the one to whom You said, "Woman, you have great faith! Your request is granted" (Matt. 15:28). Flourish this kind of faith in me, God! Help me see it coming to life as I . . .

_____

_____

_____

_____

_____

_____

_____

_____

_____

_____

_____

_____

_____

_____

_____

_____

_____

_____

_____

_____

_____

We have put our hope in the living God.
—1 Timothy 4:10

WHATEVER HE DECIDES

Therefore we do not lose heart. Though outwardly we are wasting away, yet inwardly we are being renewed day by day. For our light and momentary troubles are achieving for us an eternal glory that far outweighs them all. So we fix our eyes not on what is seen, but on what is unseen.

—*2 Corinthians 4:16-18*

Suffering is a compulsory part of human existence in a terribly fallen world. The difference for believers is that our suffering need never be in vain.

Knowing this truth sets us free. Being confident that the truth about God includes the undeniable role of suffering in our lives, that He uses it as a way of empowering and purifying His people, doesn't cause me to trust Him less. Rather, it frees me to believe Him more!

Why? Because I'm free from what scares me most about visibly, vocally proclaiming that my hope is resting entirely on Him. There have been times when I've been afraid He wouldn't come through for me, dignify me with a "yes," and prove faithful to me. But if I'm convinced that God really loves me and has certain priorities for me that may take precedence over the perceived desires of my heart, then I am safe to walk by faith.

Yes, we are safe with God—safe to believe Him for miracles, even if they come in ways we weren't expecting or didn't particularly want. Neither His dignity nor ours is at stake. We are His priority, and our trust in His sovereign will places us on the firmest ground there is.

React to the Word

Unlike anyone else, Christians are able to view earthly life in its eternal perspective, knowing that "our present sufferings are not worth comparing with the glory that will be revealed in us" (Rom. 8:18). Try placing one of your present difficulties in this hopeful light . . .

Reason with Your Heart

What kind of people would we likely be if life were always easy and upbeat?

_____

_____

_____

_____

_____

_____

_____

_____

Think of someone who's going through a difficult ordeal—one you've been through before. What would you say to them?

_____

_____

_____

_____

_____

_____

_____

_____

_____

_____

We can comfort those in any trouble with the
comfort we ourselves have received from God.
—2 Corinthians 1:4

Respond with Prayer

I desire to dwell in Your shelter, Most High. I will rest in Your shadow—the shadow of the Almighty. I will say of You, Lord, "You are my refuge and my fortress, my God, in whom I trust" (Ps. 91:1-2). Help me not be put to shame, but to be living proof of your mercy and grace, of your help and healing . . .

_____

_____

_____

_____

_____

_____

_____

_____

_____

_____

_____

_____

_____

_____

_____

_____

_____

*I want to know Christ and the power of his
resurrection and the fellowship of his sufferings.
—Philippians 3:10*

GodStops

"Savoring the Observable Presence"

I think it is right to refresh your memory.

—*2 Peter 1:13*

Remember, therefore, what you have received and heard.
—*Revelation 3:3*

My heart is stirred by a noble theme.
—Psalm 45:1

 GodStops

I will meditate on your wonders.

—Psalm 119:27

Section Three

I AM WHO
GOD SAYS I AM

Now have come the salvation and the power and the kingdom of our God, and the authority of his Christ. For the accuser of our brothers, who accuses them before our God day and night, has been hurled down. They overcame him by the blood of the Lamb and by the word of their testimony. . . . Therefore, rejoice you heavens and you who dwell in them.

—Revelation 12:10–12

IF YOU KNEW ME . . .

Moses said to God, "Who am I, that I should go to Pharaoh and bring the Israelites out of Egypt?" And God said, "I will be with you. And this will be the sign to you that it is I who have sent you: When you have brought the people out of Egypt, you will worship God on this mountain."

—Exodus 3:11–12

If I'm serious about believing God, I must believe God about me. No small challenge. Let's just say I haven't exactly been a low maintenance project for Him. I know He's omnipotent just because of the way He's kept me out of the ditch as long as He has. At lunch one day, I told my staff with much laughter that if I die suddenly, my gravestone might appropriately offer this insight into my departure: "God got tired."

I require lots of work. That's one reason why I have a little hang-up with believing "I am who God says I am." I tend to want to rewrite it as, "I strive to be who God says I am." But that's not what the Word says. It says I'm already who God says I am. And if you have received Jesus as your Savior, so are you.

I wonder if all those historical figures listed in the "Hall of Faith" (Hebrews 11) ever had trouble believing they were who God said they were? I can't answer for all of them, but Moses is a dead giveaway. The first question he asked God after he heard His voice from the burning bush was, "Who am I, that I should go to Pharaoh?"

React to the Word

If you've received Jesus as your personal Savior, the sum of your identity is found in 1 John 3:1: "How great is the love the Father has lavished on us, that we should be called the children of God! And that is what we are!" So how should your identity in Christ affect your walk today?

Reason with Your Heart

You Are Blessed—what does that mean to you?

_____

_____

_____

You Are Chosen

_____

_____

You Are Adopted

_____

_____

You Are Favored

_____

_____

You Are Redeemed

_____

_____

You Are Forgiven

_____

_____

You shine like stars in the universe.
—Philippians 2:15

Respond with Prayer

Merciful Lord, even if I were the worst of sinners (1 Tim. 1:15), as sometimes I feel I am, You still forgive me and are willing to use me. Even if I've been faithless, You've been faithful, for You cannot disown Yourself (2 Tim. 2:13). Teach me to live based on the truth of what you say about me, especially in the areas of . . .

_____

_____

_____

_____

_____

_____

_____

_____

_____

_____

_____

_____

_____

_____

_____

_____

*God will credit righteousness for us who believe
in him who raised Jesus our Lord from the dead.*
—Romans 4:24

COMING FULL CIRCLE

The LORD said to Joshua, "Today I have rolled away the reproach of Egypt from you." So the place has been called Gilgal to this day. . . . While camped at Gilgal on the plains of Jericho, the Israelites celebrated the Passover. The day after the Passover, that very day, they ate some of the produce of the land.

—Joshua 5:9–11

It was at Gilgal where, after forty years of wandering in the wilderness, the children of Israel renewed their covenant with God, subjected themselves to the rite of circumcision, and prepared their hearts for a fresh chapter of history. God presented the Israelites with a major do-over, and this time they did it right.

I'd like to suggest that Gilgal is a very important place for you and me to go, as well—a place to start over. I lived so much of my life in a cycle of defeat, this subject is very familiar to me. I really did have a heart for God, however unhealthy it may have been. My sin would always bring heartbreak, and I'd repent with all the energy I had. I'd crawl out of the pit with dirt under my nails rather than allow God to lift me out by His loving grace. And because I hadn't let Him heal my wounded heart nor ever believed I was who He said I was, sooner or later I'd cycle back into another pit.

Every believer needs second chances. We know we're coming full circle with God when we stand at a very similar crossroads where we made such a mess of life before, but this time we take a different road.

React to the Word

Christians can unfortunately experience areas of sinful captivity long after conversion. How are you coming along on your journey? Are you allowing God "to put off your old self, which is being corrupted by its deceitful desires"? (Eph. 4:22). How is He helping you in your struggle?

_____

_____

_____

_____

_____

_____

_____

_____

_____

_____

_____

_____

_____

_____

_____

_____

_____

_____

_____

Reason with Your Heart

Are you like me? Have you often lived your life in a repetitious cycle? How so?

_____

_____

_____

_____

_____

_____

_____

_____

Do you know someone else who seems trapped in this endless cycle of success and failure? How could you use your experience to help them, to walk with each other to a place of greater faithfulness, submission, and consistency?

_____

_____

_____

_____

_____

_____

_____

_____

_____

_____

The one who calls you is faithful and he will do it.
—1 Thessalonians 5:24

Respond with Prayer

Father, I thank You that if my heart has been responsive, if I have humbled myself before You, and if I have had a heart like those who tore their robes and wept in Your presence, I can know that You have heard me (2 Kings 22:19). Take this old piece of fabric from my life, roll it in the blood of Jesus, and cast it away forever . . .

For Christ, our Passover lamb, has been sacrificed..
—1 Corinthians 5:7

A GOOD PLACE TO LIVE

Remain in me, and I will remain in you. No branch can bear fruit by itself; it must remain in the vine. Neither can you bear fruit unless you remain in me. I am the vine; you are the branches. If a man remains in me and I in him, he will bear much fruit; apart from me you can do nothing.

—John 15:4-5

In pointing the children of Israel to the Promised Land, God wasn't leading them to a place they could visit. He was opening before them a place they could settle and dwell in, a place where they could live. And according to John 15, New Testament believers have likewise been called to a place of abiding. Of living. Of dwelling.

I finally came to a point in my Christian walk where I grew bone-weary of inconsistency being my only constant in life. Occasional wisps of authentic spiritual living only multiplied my frustrations. I was certain that a place of fullness and effectiveness in Christ existed, but at best I was only a drop-in. My soul needed a place it could live. I longed for my defeats to be infrequent visitations, not my victories.

Beloved, our personalized lands of earthly promise are places we're invited by God to dwell in through Christ. It's high time we stopped dropping in and started taking up residency. It's time we settled for nothing less than the blessings of citizenship, the expressions of divine favor that make life worth the bother.

React to the Word

If you think of bearing "much fruit" as a way of glorifying Christ, it changes the way you apply this promise: "If you remain in me and my words remain in you, ask whatever you wish, and it will be given you" (John 15:7). How?

_____

_____

_____

_____

_____

_____

_____

_____

_____

_____

_____

_____

_____

_____

_____

_____

_____

_____

_____

_____

_____

_____

Reason with Your Heart

You can count on this: God will accomplish His agenda regarding heaven and earth no matter what. But what difference will our believing obedience or unbelieving rebellion make on ourselves?

_____
_____
_____
_____
_____
_____
_____
_____

What difference will our faith—or our unfaith—make on our generation? On our children?

_____
_____
_____
_____
_____
_____
_____
_____

For we are God's workmanship, created in Christ Jesus to do good works, which God prepared in advance for us to do.
—Ephesians 2:10

Respond with Prayer

Father, I pray that the eyes of my heart may be enlightened in order that I may know the hope to which You have called me, the riches of Your glorious inheritance (Eph. 1:18) . . .

He has given us his very great and precious promises,
so that through them you may participate in the divine nature.
—2 Peter 1:4

TO LIVE WHAT I BELIEVE

Be strong and courageous, because you will lead these people to inherit the land I swore to their forefathers to give them. Be strong and very courageous. Be careful to obey all the law my servant Moses gave you; do not turn from it to the right or to the left, that you may be successful wherever you go.

—Joshua 1:6-7

Is it working? Your belief system, that is. Is it really working? God stated unapologetically in Joshua 1:8 that conditions exist under which we can be "prosperous and successful"—not in the self-serving sense of either of these words, but in a God-honoring demonstration of His power in a human life.

The sad part of it is, some of us are working pretty hard at something that is hardly working. Why are we doing everything we can to convince others to do something that hasn't worked terrifically well for us?

Certainly those of us who have accepted Christ as our Savior have received the automatic and glorious result of eternal salvation. We were meant, however, to be profoundly effective in letting God apply this transformation to our lives. Why have we accepted average? Are the few effects most of us see and experience all Christianity has to offer? Is this the best we can expect?

If so, someone out there needs to feel sorry for us, because for the most part, we've dumbed down New Testament Christianity and accepted our reality as theology rather than biblical theology as our reality. We've reversed the standard, walking by sight and not by faith.

React to the Word

What created in Paul the enthusiastic desire to "consider everything a loss compared to the surpassing greatness of knowing Christ Jesus my Lord"? (Phil. 3:8). How could we possess and live this hunger in our own lives?

_____

_____

_____

_____

_____

_____

_____

_____

_____

_____

_____

_____

_____

_____

_____

_____

_____

_____

_____

_____

_____

_____

_____

Reason with Your Heart

Why do you think unbelief is so much easier for us than belief?

_____

_____

_____

_____

_____

_____

_____

_____

_____

Name five things in your life that build your faith. These could be specific Scriptures, events, people, or whatever God uses to lead you to trust Him.

_____

_____

_____

_____

_____

_____

_____

_____

_____

_____

*For the LORD your God is bringing you into
a good land—a land with streams and pools of water.
—Deuteronomy 8:7*

Respond with Prayer

Father God, You have adamantly warned Your children not to be deceived (James 1:16). Am I presently being deceived in any way? If I am, please reveal it to me and give me the courage to walk in the "promised land" you have for me. Lead me to press on to that kind of life . . .

_____

_____

_____

_____

_____

_____

_____

_____

_____

_____

_____

_____

_____

_____

_____

_____

_____

_____

_____

_____

_____

His divine power has given us
everything we need for life and godliness.
—2 Peter 1:3

FOR HIGHER PURPOSES

We know that in all things God works for the good of those who love him, who have been called according to his purpose. For those God foreknew he also predestined to be conformed to the likeness of his Son, that he might be the firstborn among many brothers. And those he predestined, he also called.

—Romans 8:28-30

God is the master of multi-tasking. Look at Romans 8:28-30, and see all the things He does for us. For one thing, He has given each of us who are believers a calling. I am convinced He assigns our callings for a host of reasons, many of which serve a purpose in us, not just in those we'll serve.

For example, if God's desire was to help me face my insecurities head-on, He could not have chosen a more effective calling for me. It has certainly forced me to deal with the deeply embedded thorns of my past. He has placed me in a position where I've needed to wrestle with my fiercely handicapped identity and choose who I'd believe—Him or me.

Perhaps like some of you, I remake the decision almost every single day to believe I am who God says I am. The fact that I have not refused this public vocation is a testimony, not to me, but to the pure tenacity of God to demand that I believe Him.

Has God also placed you in a position that seems to stir up every insecurity you have? Take it personally. He is stirring it up to scoop it out . . . often one spoonful at a time.

React to the Word

"God, who has called you into fellowship with his Son Jesus Christ our Lord, is faithful" (1 Cor. 1:9). What does that tell you about the calling He has placed on your life? How sure can you be that He will fulfill it? How can you more effectively cooperate with Him in letting Him prove His faithfulness through you?

_____

_____

_____

_____

_____

_____

_____

_____

_____

_____

_____

_____

_____

_____

_____

_____

_____

_____

_____

Reason with Your Heart

In what ways does your calling accomplish more than its face value, more than meets the eye? What are some of the deeper things, the higher purposes, that God is doing through you as you serve Him?

_____

_____

_____

_____

_____

_____

_____

_____

_____

_____

_____

_____

_____

_____

_____

_____

_____

_____

_____

Put on the new self, created to be like
God in true righteousness and holiness.
—Ephesians 4:24

Respond with Prayer

Father, Your Word tells me to know assuredly that You, the Lord, have set apart the godly for Yourself. You, Lord, will hear when I call to You (Ps. 4:3). You, Lord, understand all about me, yet You love me—and Your love causes You to continue working on me until I am more and more like You. Help me, Father, to embrace this calling . . .

_____

_____

_____

_____

_____

_____

_____

_____

_____

_____

_____

_____

_____

_____

_____

_____

_____

_____

*I have set you apart from
the nations to be my own.*
—Leviticus 20:26

GodStops

"Savoring the Observable Presence"

At the LORD's command, Moses recorded the stages in their journey.
—*Numbers 33:2*

Son of man, record this date, this very date.
—Ezekiel 24:2

Write them on the doorframes of your houses and on your gates.
—Deuteronomy 6:9

Remember those earlier days . . . when you stood your ground.
—Hebrews 10:32

Section four

I CAN DO
ALL THINGS
THROUGH CHRIST

During the fourth watch of the night Jesus went out to them, walking on the lake. When the disciples saw him walking on the lake, they were terrified. "It's a ghost," they said, and cried out in fear. But Jesus immediately said to them: "Take courage! It is I. Don't be afraid." "Lord, if it's you," Peter replied, "tell me to come to you on the water." "Come," he said.

—Matthew 14:25-29

THE POWER OF ONE

The LORD said to Joshua son of Nun, Moses' aide: "Moses my servant is dead. Now then, you and all these people, get ready to cross the Jordan River into the land I am about to give to them—to the Israelites. I will give you every place where you set your foot, as I promised Moses."

—Joshua 1:1-3

You really can do it, you know. Whatever the harrowing path before you, you really can walk it victoriously. God will give you every place you step your feet for the glory of His name if you let Him.

How do I know? For starters, Philippians 4:13 claims that a servant of God can do "all things" through Christ who gives him strength. That includes the otherwise impossible, which is why the statement "I can do all things through Christ" isn't just a cheer or a feel-good memory verse. It is sound theology yearning to become our reality.

It's not as though God mightily uses only a few chosen people in each generation and everyone else is basically insignificant. Under the inspiration of the Holy Spirit, Paul stressed the importance of the whole body of believers working together. Furthermore, he stated that "those parts of the body that seem to be weaker are indispensable, and the parts that we think are less honorable we treat with special honor" (1 Cor. 12:22).

Christ left us too much to do to leave it up to a few. You are an honored part of the body of Christ, and your contributions add up.

React to the Word

What does it mean to you that Jesus said: "I tell you the truth, anyone who has faith in me will do what I have been doing. He will do even greater things than these, because I am going to the Father"? (John 14:12). Personalize this to your own life.

_____

_____

_____

_____

_____

_____

_____

_____

_____

_____

_____

_____

_____

_____

_____

_____

_____

_____

_____

_____

Reason with Your Heart

What do you need to do to get the enemy off your Promised Land?

With what does Satan most often attack you? Fear? Discouragement? What makes his method effective? How can you better counteract it?

Do not be terrified; do not be discouraged.

—Joshua 1:9

Respond with Prayer

God, enable me to stand firm, with the belt of truth buckled around my waist and with the breastplate of righteousness in place (Eph. 6:14). Help me to understand that without the girding of truth, I am defenseless against the devil. Truth is my main defense against the father of lies. I believe today that You can help me to . . .

_____

_____

_____

_____

_____

_____

_____

_____

_____

_____

_____

_____

_____

_____

_____

_____

_____

I will boast all the more gladly about my weaknesses,
so that Christ's power may rest on me.
—2 Corinthians 12:9

WHATEVER YOU SAY

With the tongue we praise our Lord and Father, and with it we curse men, who have been made in God's likeness. Out of the same mouth come praise and cursing. My brothers, this should not be. Can both fresh water and salt water flow from the same spring?

—*James 3:9–11*

Imagine what could happen if we allowed God to take authority of our mouths and infuse our words with His power. Think about the positive impact we could have on our circumstances, our mates, our children, our neighbors, our coworkers, our friends, and those we serve.

Scripture tells us that if Christ's words dwell in us, the Holy Spirit will often affect powerful results through us when we pray and speak what we believe. The tongue itself is merely a muscle, of course. It doesn't have any supernatural power of its own. But when we as Christians "believe and therefore speak" (2 Cor. 4:13), the Holy Spirit can use our tongues as instruments or vessels of supernatural power and bring about stunning results, whether immediately or over time.

God is not, however, nearly as likely to powerfully and regularly infuse an instrument that is also employed for opposing purposes. In other words, the wrong use of the instrument can dramatically hinder its effectiveness. But no matter how stubborn the tongue nor how habitual our problem, God can sanctify it and make it a vessel of honor and power.

React to the Word

Luke 6:45 says, "For out of the overflow of his heart his mouth speaks." How does a wayward tongue signal a wayward heart? What have you noticed about the words that come to your lips during times of disobedience? What about during times of faithfulness?

_____

_____

_____

_____

_____

_____

_____

_____

_____

_____

_____

_____

_____

_____

_____

_____

_____

_____

_____

_____

_____

Reason with Your Heart

Why is nothing a greater threat to the enemy than a believer with the Word of God living and active upon her tongue?

Name as many of Christ's New Testament commands that involve the tongue as you can. How can we respond to these in obedience?

If anyone is never at fault in what he says,
he is a perfect man, able to keep his whole body in check.
—James 3:2

Respond with Prayer

Father, I approach your throne of grace with confidence, so that I may receive mercy and find grace to help me in this particular need (Heb. 4:16). Knowing that the same grace which saves me also sanctifies, I come seeking a fresh work of consecration . . .

See, this has touched your lips;
your guilt is taken away and your sin atoned for.
—Isaiah 6:7

LIVING LOVE

Be imitators of God, therefore, as dearly loved children and live a life of love, just as Christ loved us and gave himself up for us as a fragrant offering and sacrifice to God.

—Ephesians 5:1-2

God placed such a high priority on believing Him, it seems impossible to try prioritizing the other actions and practices that make up Christian living. Under the inspiration of the Holy Spirit, however, a two-pronged priority floated to the top for the Apostle Paul. He wrote, "The only thing that counts is faith expressing itself through love" (Gal. 5:6).

Faith and love. Faith is God's invitation to make the impossible possible. He is greatly glorified when He enables us to do something we're unable to do ourselves. And I can think of few things further beyond our capabilities than this: loving those we don't want to love . . . or don't even like.

If we place 2 Corinthians 5:7 (which tells us to live by faith and not by sight) next to Galatians 5:6, we come up with two life challenges that, if accepted, could catapult us onto a path infinitely higher than this world's self-centered interstate of mediocrity: We live by faith. We love by faith.

We are literally to live love. Fuzzy thought, isn't it? Not according to Ephesians 5:2, which says that the very nature of love is sacrificial. In fact, if we're not presently feeling the squeeze and sacrifice of loving, we're probably exercising a preferential, highly selective, self-centered human substitute.

React to the Word

Recognizing that love is more often an act of the will than of the heart, how do you react when we're succinctly told in 1 Corinthians 13:8 that love never fails? Have you ever known love to fail? Have you tried loving someone only to see it come to nothing?

Reason with Your Heart

How is loving someone by faith different than loving them by human effort?

_____

_____

_____

_____

_____

_____

_____

_____

What happens if you expend untold, self-sacrificing efforts toward someone for years without seeing any apparent fruit? Anything good?

_____

_____

_____

_____

_____

_____

_____

_____

_____

*Hope does not disappoint us, because God has poured
out his love into our hearts by the Holy Spirit.*
—Romans 5:5

Respond with Prayer

Lord, I have heard that it was said, "Love your neighbor and hate your enemy." But You tell me to love my enemies and pray for those who persecute me, that I might be a child of my Father in heaven (Matt. 5:43-44). Show me how, Lord . . .

_____

_____

_____

_____

_____

_____

_____

_____

_____

_____

_____

_____

_____

_____

_____

_____

_____

_____

_____

_____

If we love one another, God lives in us
and his love is made complete in us.
—1 John 4:12

THE SHIELD OF FAITH

Our struggle is not against flesh and blood, but against the rulers, against the authorities, against the powers of this dark world and against the spiritual forces of evil in the heavenly realms. Therefore put on the full armor of God.

—*Ephesians 6:12–13*

Just like the children of Israel, we will always have an enemy who wants to keep us out of our Promised Lands. So if we're going to win our battles, we're going to have to wise up to some of Satan's schemes and prepare in advance for victory.

The first part of Ephesians 6:16 (KJV) tells us, "Above all, taking the shield of faith . . . ye shall be able to quench all the fiery darts of the wicked."

Why "above all" do we need to learn to use our "shield of faith"? Because the shield is the armor's armor. If Satan can get us to drop our shield of faith, he knows we can't remain standing for very long.

Our toughest battles will invariably concern matters of faith: times when we're tempted to think God's Word and His ways won't work for us, that He has abandoned us, let us down, or failed to come through for us. This is why "above all," you and I need to take up our shield of faith. When we respond to attacks of doubt, distortion, and deceit by raising the shield of faith and speaking the truth of God's Word, the fiery dart is extinguished and the enemy takes another hit.

React to the Word

In the Eden temptation (Genesis 3:1-6), what were the first words out of Satan's mouth? Why were they so effective? Think about the last time you heard this: "I know what the Bible says about (fill in the blank) . . . but . . ." Do you spot the danger in that statement?

_____

_____

_____

_____

_____

_____

_____

_____

_____

_____

_____

_____

_____

_____

_____

_____

_____

_____

_____

_____

Reason with Your Heart

What influences in your life have discouraged you from trusting God, from believing God?

_____

_____

_____

_____

_____

_____

_____

_____

How could trusting God help you to battle back against Satan's attacks on your life?

_____

_____

_____

_____

_____

_____

_____

_____

Resist him, standing firm in the faith.

—1 Peter 5:9

Respond with Prayer

According to Your Word, if I'm really going to be one of your disciples, I must hold to Your teaching. Then I will know the truth, and the truth will set me free (John 8:31-32). Help me to see this vital link between Your truth and my liberty. . . .

Fight the good fight of the faith. Take hold of the eternal life.
—1 Timothy 6:12

FAITH WORKS

When [Jesus] had gone indoors, the blind men came to him, and he asked them, "Do you believe that I am able to do this?" "Yes, Lord," they replied. Then he touched their eyes and said, "According to your faith will it be done to you."

—Matthew 9:28–29

Nothing works like faith. Its God-ordained dividends are astronomical. Unfortunately, so are the costs of its absence. Biblically speaking, the reason why faith is without equal in its effects upon the human life is precisely because God is without equal—and because when we invite Him into our lives by faith, He answers with proof of His power.

If faith works, then, we should want to make sure we know what faith is. In New Testament Greek, the word used for "faith" is *pistis*, which means assurance, belief, faith, fidelity. That's why when I use the phrase "Believing God," you can think of it interchangeably with "having faith in God."

Christ can operate any way He desires, but His usual mode of operation regarding His followers is this: "According to your faith will it be done to you." Whether or not we like the concept, Christ loves to respond to us according to our faith.

I used to bristle over this idea—until I started exercising a little more belief and began experiencing completely unexpected and exceeding results. I've noted a pretty reliable ratio along the way: the less faith we have, the more we tend to resent the concept.

React to the Word

"Rise and go; your faith has made you well" (Luke 17:19). How do you respond to the suggestion that God's action may be determined by your faith?

_____

_____

_____

_____

_____

_____

_____

_____

_____

_____

_____

_____

_____

_____

_____

_____

_____

_____

_____

_____

_____

_____

Reason with Your Heart

Why do you suppose Jesus often connected His miracles to the person's faith?

_____

_____

_____

_____

_____

_____

_____

How would you respond to the person who says that God will do what He wants . . . with or without our faith?

_____

_____

_____

_____

_____

_____

_____

_____

_____

Jesus turned and saw her. "Take heart, daughter,"
he said, "your faith has healed you."
—Matthew 9:22

Respond with Prayer

You asked in Your Word, Lord, "When the Son of Man comes, will He find faith on the earth?" (Luke 18:8). You search the world over for people with faith. Make me one of them, Lord. Teach me to trust You with an expectant faith when I am tempted to doubt.

"Where is your faith?" he asked his disciples.

—Luke 8:25

 GodStops

"Savoring the Observable Presence"

Be careful that you do not forget the LORD.
—Deuteronomy 6:12

List my tears on your scroll—are they not on your record?
—Psalm 56:8

Even now my witness is in heaven; my advocate is on high.
—Job 16:19

It is no trouble for me to write the same things to you again.
—Philippians 3:1

Section five

GOD'S WORD IS ALIVE AND ACTIVE IN ME

The law of the LORD is perfect, reviving the soul. The statutes of the LORD are trustworthy, making wise the simple. The precepts of the LORD are right, giving joy to the heart. The commands of the LORD are radiant, giving light to the eyes. . . . By them is your servant warned; in keeping them there is great reward.

—Psalm 19:7-8, 11

THE WORD COMES TO LIFE

 For the word of God is living and active. Sharper than any double-edged sword, it penetrates even to dividing soul and spirit, joints and marrow; it judges the thoughts and attitudes of the heart.

—Hebrews 4:12

Don't miss the crucial tie between the Word of God and the people of God in this verse. God not only told us His Word is alive, effective, and powerful on its own. He insisted that it has supernatural effects for those who receive it by faith.

When we receive the Word by reading it, meditating on it, believing it, and applying it, the life of the Word becomes lively in us. The power and activity of the Word become active in us. The operations and energy of the Word become energizing in us. The effectiveness of the Word becomes effective in us. In fact, according to Hebrews 4:12, when we receive God's Word, it invades every part of our being, even the marrow of our bones and the motives of our hearts.

God doesn't speak to hear the sound of His voice or to be heard by others. God says His Word "will not return to me empty, but will accomplish what I desire and achieve the purpose for which I sent it" (Isa. 55:11). God's Word possesses accomplishing power and achieving power. That's a fact. And I want it to have the same accomplishing and achieving power in me.

React to the Word

"Pay attention to what I say; listen closely to my words. Do not let them out of your sight, keep them within your heart; for they are life to those who find them and health to a man's whole body" (Prov. 4:20-22). *How can these words of Scripture operate in your life? Have you ever experienced the Word changing you from the inside out?*

Reason with Your Heart

How great has your expectation of God's Word been in your life?

What can you deliberately do, not just to read God's Word, but to receive it like a famished person at a feast?

Your words came, I ate them; they were my joy and my heart's delight.
—Jeremiah 15:16

Respond with Prayer

Father, I ask You to help me receive the Word of God, not as the word of men, but as it actually is—the Word of God—which is actively at work in those who believe (1 Thess. 2:13). Make it effective in me today, and make me effective in You . . .

_____

_____

_____

_____

_____

_____

_____

_____

_____

_____

_____

_____

_____

_____

_____

_____

Let the word of Christ dwell in you richly.
—Colossians 3:16

SAY IT LIKE YOU MEAN IT

 When we put bits into the mouths of horses to make them obey us, we can turn the whole animal. Or take ships as an example. Although they are so large and are driven by strong winds, they are steered by a very small rudder wherever the pilot wants to go. Likewise the tongue is a small part of the body.

—James 3:3-5

Mankind possesses uniqueness among all other creatures because we were created in the image of God. Our unique ability to communicate through words is one of the most obvious evidences of the image we bear. The Scripture even calls Christ "the Word" that "became flesh, and dwelt among us" (John 1:14).

By virtue of being created in our divine Communicator's image, I'd like to suggest that our words—not just God's—also possess an element of accomplishing and achieving power. Proverbs 18:21 says, "The tongue has the power of life and death." The application of this verse is primarily figurative (with the exception of kings, judges, and dictators), but make no mistake— words are far from diminutive. We possess no small power in our tongues.

Most of us can testify that the human tongue owns the power to kill all sorts of things. Relationships, lifelong dreams, and self-confidence are only a few of the common fatalities. Thankfully, however, perhaps as many of us have also experienced life-giving words of encouragement, instruction, and exhortation. Words like these are ours from God to give.

React to the Word

Before God told Joshua to meditate on His Word and live by its precepts, He issued this command: "Do not let this Book of the Law depart from your mouth" (Josh. 1:8). What did God mean? How does this strike you? How can we do this?

_____

_____

_____

_____

_____

_____

_____

_____

_____

_____

_____

_____

_____

_____

_____

_____

_____

_____

Reason with Your Heart

How do you respond to the suggestion that we have no greater built-in vessel to express divine power than our mouths?

_____

_____

_____

_____

_____

_____

_____

_____

What lengths do you think Satan will go to set the tongue of a believer aflame with the fire of hell? How have you witnessed this happening?

_____

_____

_____

_____

_____

_____

_____

_____

_____

Above all else, guard your heart, for it is the wellspring of life.
—Proverbs 4:23

Respond with Prayer

Lord, according to Scripture, the Word is near me; it is in my mouth and in my heart, and it is the word of faith that I am proclaiming (Rom. 10:8). Cause me to continue to listen to Your Word! Without it, my faith and belief will never grow. Teach me, Lord . . .

Humbly accept the word planted in you, which can save you.

—James 1:21

FAITHFUL FOOTSTEPS

March around the city once with all the armed men. Do this for six days. . . . On the seventh day, march around the city seven times, with the priests blowing the trumpets. When you hear them sound a long blast on the trumpets, have all the people give a loud shout; then the wall of the city will collapse.
—Joshua 6:3-5

Joshua might have thought, "Lord, why march around the city for six days, then seven more times on the seventh day? Can't we just shout on Day One and see the walls collapse?" At least, that's what most of the Israelites were probably thinking. Wanting it now is not a purely modern idea.

I am confident we can still believe God for something dramatic and miraculous. But in between dramatic revelations, what's a believer to do? The day-in, day-out fundamentals—like prayer, a daily time in God's Word, praise and worship, attending church, serving others, giving. These are the fundamentals, and they'll never change.

We can make all the excuses in the world for not practicing these, but they represent the backbone of obedience. We often want the mystical while God is insisting on the practical. We may want a constant dose of dramatics, but God enjoys seeing the perseverance and faithfulness of simple, daily devotion.

Sometimes the greatest proof of God's miraculous power occurs when an attention-deficit-seeker-of-instant-gratification denies himself, takes up his cross, and follows Christ . . . for the long haul.

React to the Word

"Let us not become weary in doing good, for at the proper time we will reap a harvest if we do not give up" (Gal. 6:9). How does this passage encourage you to stay faithful? How have you experienced the long-term benefits of this wise perspective?

Reason with Your Heart

How do you react to the picture of God nudging you and me awake before dawn because He can hardly wait to be with us?

_____

_____

_____

_____

_____

_____

_____

_____

What day-in, day-out fundamentals make up your daily relationship with God? Which ones do you wish most to acquire and perfect?

_____

_____

_____

_____

_____

_____

_____

_____

_____

I have seen you in the sanctuary
and beheld your power and your glory.
—Psalm 63:2

Respond with Prayer

O Lord, You have made everything beautiful in Your time. You have also set eternity in the hearts of men; yet we cannot fathom what You have done from beginning to end (Ecc. 3:11). Allow my faithfulness to fan the flame of Your desire to show me Your glory.

_____

_____

_____

_____

_____

_____

_____

_____

_____

_____

_____

_____

_____

_____

_____

_____

Be exalted, O God, above the heavens;
let your glory be over all the earth.
—Psalm 57:5

PRESENT ACTIVE PARTICIPLE

Having believed, you were marked in him with a seal, the promised Holy Spirit. . . . I pray also that the eyes of your heart may be enlightened in order that you may know the hope to which he has called you, the riches of his glorious inheritance . . . and his incomparably great power for us who believe.

—Ephesians 1:13, 18–19

Paul used two very important and distinctive verb tenses of the same basic word "believe" in verses 13 and 19. Verse 13 speaks of Christians "having believed." This faith-action was exercised in the *past* with obviously radical results—salvation.

The Greek verb tense of "believe" in verse 19, however, is called a *present active participle.* As one of my Greek instructors explained it to me: "Beth, when you see a present active participle Greek verb, you can think of the word 'continually' preceding the verb." In other words, the promise given in Ephesians 1:18-21 is not applied to those "having believed"—the ones who were included in verse 13. Rather it is applied to those who are presently, actively, and, yes, continually believing God.

My point? Our glorious walk with God began with an act of faith that brought us into relationship with Jesus Christ as our Savior. But it doesn't end there. God is calling you and me to leave the life of passivity bred by a past-tense view of faith. He wants us to get caught in the act of present-active-participle believing.

React to the Word

"Even though you do not see him now, you believe in him and are filled with an inexpressible and glorious joy, for you are receiving the goal of your faith, the salvation of your souls" (1 Pet. 1:8-9). Yes, we've been saved. And yes, we will be saved. But how are you experiencing God saving you today, every day?

_____

_____

_____

_____

_____

_____

_____

_____

_____

_____

_____

_____

_____

_____

_____

_____

_____

_____

_____

Reason with Your Heart

Describe at least three current situations in your life where you have the opportunity to actively believe God.

_____

_____

_____

_____

_____

_____

_____

_____

_____

If you do believe God in the situations you mentioned—rather than trusting yourself, something, or someone else—how do you expect they will turn out?

_____

_____

_____

_____

_____

_____

_____

_____

_____

_____

_____

We take captive every thought to make it obedient to Christ.
—2 Corinthians 10:5

Respond with Prayer

Lord God, You don't want me to be persuaded just by the words of men. You want me to be persuaded by the demonstration of the Spirit's power, so that my faith will not rest on men's wisdom but on Your power (1 Cor. 2:4-5). Teach me to trust Your incomparably great power for the needs in my life . . .

_____

_____

_____

_____

_____

_____

_____

_____

_____

_____

_____

_____

_____

_____

_____

_____

Then we will no longer be infants, tossed back and forth by the waves, and blown here and there by every wind of teaching.
—Ephesians 4:14

BELIEVING GOD EVER AFTER

 Beyond all question, the mystery of godliness is great: He appeared in a body, was vindicated by the Spirit, was seen by angels, was preached among the nations, was believed on in the world, was taken up in glory.

—1 Timothy 3:16

Reflect back on the five statements from our pledge of faith:

- *God is who He says He is,*
- *God can do what He says He can do,*
- *I am who God says I am,*
- *I can do all things through Christ,* and
- *God's Word is alive and active in me.*

These are always true, and He is always faithful.

Thank you, dear one, for the joy of your company along this path of faith. I will never forget this *Believing God* adventure as long as I live. If you're like me, you desperately needed a little sound biblical permission to take God at His Word. How I pray you've received that . . . for "without faith it is impossible to please God" (Heb. 11:6).

I'd like to "believe and therefore speak" a few appropriate blessings over you: 1) May the timeline of your life stay straight and steady. 2) May your eyes remain fixed on Jesus, the author and finisher of your faith, who awaits you at your finish line. 3) May the path between your today and your eternity be strewn with stones of remembrance.

React to the Word

What impact does 1 John 5:14 have on your faith walk? "This is the confidence which we have before Him, that, if we ask anything according to His will, He hears us."

Reason with Your Heart

What memorial stones can you erect to remind you that Christ has helped you thus far in your journey?

_____
_____
_____
_____
_____
_____
_____
_____

How will reminding yourself of God's faithfulness help you believe Him for the future?

_____
_____
_____
_____
_____
_____
_____
_____

Samuel took a stone . . . [and] named it Ebenezer,
saying, "Thus far has the LORD helped us."
—1 Samuel 7:12

Respond with Prayer

O Lord, I want You to be able to say of me, "I know your deeds, your love and faith, your service and perseverance, and that you are now doing more than you did at first" (Rev. 2:19). Teach me to make each day an invitation to a new beginning and a day of fresh commitment.

You believe at last!

—John 16:31

GodStops

"Savoring the Observable Presence"

Let us fix our eyes on Jesus.
——*Hebrews 12:2*

This I call to mind and therefore I have hope.

—Lamentations 3:21

 GodStops

_____

_____

_____

_____

_____

_____

_____

_____

_____

_____

_____

_____

_____

_____

_____

_____

_____

_____

_____

_____

_____

_____

_____

_____

_____

_____

_____

_____

_____

How priceless is your unfailing love!
—Psalm 36:7

I will sing of the LORD's great love forever.
—Psalm 89:1